BEYOND THE ABYSS

A SUBTERRANEAN ADVENTURE

Vivaan Jay Ahir

NEXUS STORIES PUBLICATION®

Surat, Gujarat, India.

Title – Beyond the Abyss

First Published by Nexus Stories Publication 2023

Copyright © Vivaan Jay Ahir 2023

All Rights Reserved.

ISBN # 978-81-19178-52-0

Publication
Nexus Stories Publication™, Surat (Gujarat), Bhārata
www.nexus-stories.com | +91 87800 80718 | www.nexus-stories.in

TO,

____

____

WITH LOVE,

FROM

____

____

Index

1 ❋ The Call of the Cryptic Map

In the quaint town of Ethervale, where misty mountains cradled the horizon, the protagonist, a young and curious soul named Aiden, lived an ordinary life. But an insatiable longing for adventure lurked within his heart, sparked by the enchanting stories whispered by the village elders. Tales of ancient civilizations, hidden artifacts, and the mysterious underground world ignited a relentless curiosity that could no longer be ignored.

One fateful evening, while exploring the dusty attic of their family home, Aiden stumbled upon a worn and weathered parchment tucked between old books and forgotten trinkets. Unfurling it, he discovered an intricately drawn map, its surface covered in cryptic symbols and markings. The map was like a riddle, tantalizing and elusive, leaving Aiden wondering about its origin and purpose.

As night fell, Aiden couldn't shake the allure of the map. He knew deep within that this was the beginning of an extraordinary journey, one that would forever change their destiny. The prospect of delving into the underground world and uncovering its secrets was too compelling to resist.

Determined to unlock the map's secrets, Aiden sought out like-minded souls who shared his thirst for adventure. One by one, he gathered a group of companions, each with their unique talents and aspirations. Among them were Maya, an archaeologist with an insatiable curiosity about the past; Kael, a charming rogue with a penchant for uncovering lost treasures; Elara, a wise sage whose knowledge of ancient lore was unparalleled; and Gideon, a steadfast and loyal warrior bound by honour and duty.

Aiden's voice tinged with excitement as they exclaimed, "Look, Maya, Kael, Elara, Gideon! I found something extraordinary! This map holds the secrets of the underground world. The stories we've heard could be true, and the artifacts we seek might be hidden beneath the surface!"

Maya, the archaeologist, leaned in, her eyes shining with curiosity. "Fascinating! These symbols seem ancient, and the intricate patterns suggest a hidden labyrinth of tunnels."

Kael, the charming rogue, flashed a smile. "Ah, an adventure awaits us then! Count me in for uncovering lost treasures and ancient mysteries."

Elara, the wise sage, nodded sagely. "The underground world is full of wonders and dangers. But if we tread carefully, we might uncover its forgotten past."

Gideon, the steadfast warrior, spoke with determination, "This journey will not be without peril, but with you all by my side, I fear no darkness."

With a shared sense of purpose, the group examined the map, pooling their expertise to decipher its enigmatic symbols. Gradually, patterns emerged, revealing a series of interconnected paths leading deep into the heart of the underground world.

Maya's eyes sparkled with excitement. "This is a once-in-a-lifetime opportunity! The artifacts we could discover could rewrite history!"

Kael chuckled, a glint of mischief in his eyes. "And think of the riches we might find! The treasures of the underground world are bound to be priceless."

Elara's expression turned serious. "Remember, the artifacts we seek could hold immense power. We must approach this quest with caution and wisdom."

Gideon nodded, his hand resting on his sword. "Agreed. We must remain vigilant. Danger lurks in the shadows."

Determined to unlock the map's secrets, Aiden sought out like-minded souls who shared their thirst for adventure. One by one, they gathered a group of companions, each with their unique talents and aspirations.

Maya adjusted her glasses, a glint of excitement in her eyes. "I've always dreamt of uncovering the mysteries of the past. This quest could be the breakthrough we need in the field of archaeology."

Kael grinned, twirling a lock of his dark hair. "Well, if there are ancient relics to be found, you can count me in. It'll be like a game of hide-and-seek with history."

Elara's presence radiated calm wisdom. "We must approach this journey with reverence. The underground world holds secrets beyond our comprehension."

Gideon stood tall; his hands clenched into fists. "I'll protect you all, no matter what dangers we face. We must remain united."

As they stood at the entrance of the hidden underground world, a sense of trepidation washed over them. The cavern's yawning darkness seemed to swallow them whole, but their shared resolve shone like a beacon amidst the shadows.

Aiden stepped forward, clutching the cryptic map tightly in their hands. With a deep breath, they took the first step, and the others followed, united by a sense of camaraderie and a shared quest for ancient artifacts.

Maya's voice carried a sense of wonder as she murmured, "This is like stepping into history itself. I can't believe we're embarking on such a journey."

Kael chuckled softly, his steps light and nimble. "I knew life had more in store for me than just tavern brawls and petty thievery. Let's make history together!"

Elara's eyes gleamed with a mix of anticipation and caution. "The underground world is known for its riddles and trials. Stay vigilant, my friends."

Gideon's presence was a comforting anchor in the darkness. "No matter what lies ahead, we'll face it together. As a team."

With every discovery, the group unravelled fragments of the past etched into the underground's architecture and artifacts. Each revelation felt like a piece of a puzzle, shedding light on a forgotten era & hinting at the profound connection between the past and their present reality.

Maya's hands traced the delicate engravings on an ancient stone tablet. "This script is like nothing I've seen before. It must hold an important message."

Kael's fingers danced over a hidden lever, revealing a concealed passage. "Ah, secrets are hidden in plain sight. I like this underground world more and more."

Elara's gaze lingered on the murals adorning the cavern walls. "These depictions tell tales of an ancient civilization's triumphs and tragedies."

Gideon's sword gleamed in the dim light as he stood guard. "Stay close, everyone. We don't know what creatures or traps might be lurking."

Maya's voice was tinged with contemplation. "We must be cautious with these artifacts. Their power could change the course of history."

Kael's eyes widened, pondering the implications. "True. We need to consider the consequences of our actions."

Elara's wisdom shone through her words. "Power can be a double-edged sword. We must use it responsibly."

Gideon's voice was resolute. "Our hearts must guide us, and we must remember our purpose — protecting the realm above."

Yet they pressed on.

2 ✤ The Oracle's Revelation

The group huddles around the campfire, their faces illuminated by its flickering glow, as they recount their individual experiences from their journey into the depths of the underground world. Maya, the archaeologist, speaks first, her eyes filled with wonder, "I saw a grand city, ancient and majestic, standing tall amidst a thriving civilization. It was as if time itself had frozen in awe of their ingenuity and wisdom."

Kael, the charismatic rogue, grins, "Ah, and I stumbled upon treasures that sparkled like stars in the darkness. But now, after hearing all your tales, those trinkets seem insignificant compared to the importance of our quest."

Elara, the wise sage, adds, "I, too, was touched by ancient wisdom, fragments of knowledge that resonate deep within me. These insights are guiding us, shaping the choices we make on this journey."

Gideon, the valiant warrior, recalls his visions, "I saw great battles fought to protect the sacred artifacts we seek. It's clear that the artifacts are not just objects of power; they hold the key to averting the impending catastrophe."

The companions fall into contemplative silence as the weight of their quest settles upon them. They now understand that their journey holds greater significance than they initially realized. It is not merely about collecting artifacts but about preserving the wisdom of an ancient civilization and safeguarding the world from an impending cataclysm.

Each revelation sparks introspection, and the companions share their thoughts and fears. They realize that the power they seek could easily be misused, and the burden of making the right choices weighs heavily on their minds. But they also find solace in their shared bond, knowing that together, they can navigate the challenges that lie ahead.

As the group delves deeper into the underground world, their exploration yields more ancient artifacts, each adding a piece to the puzzle of the prophecy's message. They decipher inscriptions, interpret symbols, and immerse themselves in the stories the artifacts tell, gaining insight into the ancient civilization's values and beliefs.

Their journey is not without obstacles. Adversaries appear to thwart them at every turn, coveting the artifacts' power for their selfish ends. Cunning rogues attempt to outmanoeuvre Kael, while malevolent sorcerers seek to exploit Elara's knowledge of ancient lore. The companions face each threat with unwavering unity and resourcefulness, their shared bond proving to be their greatest strength.

One fateful encounter leads them to a cloaked figure — an enigmatic stranger who claims to be a lone survivor from ancient civilization. The stranger's eyes hold the wisdom of ages as they share tales of the artifacts' history and the consequences that await if they fall into the wrong hands.

The stranger's words echo in the companions' minds, deepening their ethical dilemma. They realize the immense power of the relics could either bring salvation or plunge their world into ruin. The weight of such a momentous choice threatens to fracture the unity they hold so dear.

Yet, amidst the challenges and dilemmas, the companions find glimmers of hope. The underground world reveals remnants of the ancient civilization's benevolence — a testament to their capacity for compassion and selflessness. These moments inspire the group to seek a path that harnesses the artifacts' power for the greater good, preserving the delicate balance between the realms and ensuring a brighter future for all.

The companions draw strength from each other, reaffirming their shared commitment to the quest's noble purpose. They resolve to protect the underground world's secrets, preserving the wisdom of the past for generations to come. With newfound clarity, they face the daunting journey ahead, steadfast in their belief that their choices will shape not only their destinies but the fate of their world.

In the heart of the underground world, the group stands united, their spirits kindled by the oracle's revelations and the knowledge they've gained. As they continue their journey, guided by the visions and the legacy of the hidden chamber, they remain resolute in their pursuit of the ancient artifacts and the path they must tread to safeguard their world from impending calamity. The trials that lie ahead may be daunting, but their shared purpose and unwavering determination will carry them through the subterranean depths, toward a destiny they are yet to uncover.

3 ✦ Resonance of the Past

In the heart of the underground world, the companions followed the haunting echoes that seemed to reverberate through time itself. Each step drew them closer to the remnants of an ancient civilization, where the secrets of the abyss awaited to be uncovered.

As they ventured deeper into the underground tunnels, the group found themselves in a vast chamber adorned with mesmerizing murals. The echoes guided their gaze to the artwork, and scenes from a bygone era came to life before their eyes. They witnessed a civilization that revered the underground world, living in harmony with its mysteries and holding a profound connection to its depths.

Aiden marvelled at the artwork, "These murals tell a story of a civilization that understood the beauty and wisdom of this underground realm. They saw it as more than just darkness; it was a source of knowledge and enlightenment."

Maya nodded in agreement, "It's fascinating how they celebrated the underground with such reverence. It's like they had a deep understanding of its significance in their lives."

The companions continued their exploration, encountering awe-inspiring architectural wonders.

Underground cathedrals with majestic pillars, intricate passageways adorned with elaborate carvings, and statues depicting mythical creatures left them in awe of the ancient civilization's ingenuity and craftsmanship.

Kael admired the craftsmanship, "Look at these carvings! It's incredible how they've preserved their history through such intricate art."

Elara studied the inscriptions, her eyes bright with curiosity, "The writings on the walls tell stories of their beliefs and values. It's like we're uncovering a lost civilization's diary."

With a sense of wonder and curiosity, the companions deciphered inscriptions etched into the walls. The ancient writings revealed fragments of profound wisdom, portraying a civilization that saw the underground world not as a dark abyss but as a wellspring of knowledge, spirituality, and enlightenment.

Gideon mused, "Their understanding of the underground's significance runs deep. It's as if they knew the secrets that lie beneath the surface."

Throughout their journey, the group encountered statues and relics dedicated to the guardians of the abyss. These revered beings, depicted as protectors of wisdom and gatekeepers of the underground realm, left an indelible impression on the companions, hinting at a profound connection between the ancient civilization and the depths they inhabited.

Maya observed, "These statues represent more than just physical protection. They symbolize a deep sense of guardianship over the underground world."

Following the echoes, the companions arrived at ancient ritual sites where ceremonial practices once took place. The echoes of the past seemed to envelop them, and they felt the reverberations of sacred rites conducted in reverence for the underground's mystical powers.

Kael whispered, "Do you feel that? It's like the echoes are carrying us back in time, allowing us to witness these rituals firsthand."

As they immersed themselves in the echoes of the past, the group began to understand that the ancient civilization lived in harmony with the underground world. The echoes carried a message of respect and understanding — a profound connection that once united two realms, bridging the gap between the surface and the depths.

Elara spoke with awe, "Their rituals demonstrate a deep bond with the underground world. They saw it as a source of spiritual connection and enlightenment."

Amidst their admiration for the past, the companions also encountered evidence of a cataclysm that befell the ancient civilization. Signs of devastation told a haunting tale of a tragic event that disrupted the delicate balance between the surface and the depths, providing a cautionary reminder of the consequences of disturbing this equilibrium.

Aiden's voice turned sombre, "It's a reminder that we must tread carefully. The choices we make can either preserve the harmony or upset the balance of the realms."

The echoes became more than just a haunting sound; they offered valuable lessons from history. The companions came to understand that their quest was not solely about acquiring artifacts but about safeguarding the balance that once prevailed and preserving the ancient civilization's legacy.

Maya said thoughtfully, "The echoes are like a guide, leading us to discover the wisdom and lessons of the past. We must learn from them to shape our future."

Strengthened by the resonance of the past, the group found a deeper sense of unity and shared destiny. They acknowledged the responsibility bestowed upon them, knowing that their actions would shape their world's future and the legacy of the underground civilization.

Gideon added, "Our bond as companions is essential. We must support each other on this journey, for our choices will impact not only ourselves but the entire world above and below."

The echoes also served as a mirror, reflecting the companions' own beliefs, fears, and desires. Each member confronted their vulnerabilities and uncertainties, finding strength in the knowledge that their unity and purpose were vital in the face of challenges.

Elara revealed, "I see my fears mirrored in these echoes, but I also find solace in knowing that we face these challenges together."

Fuelled by the echoes' revelations, the group sought answers from the artifacts, murals, and inscriptions. They yearned to discern the events that led to the past's downfall, hoping to unravel the truth behind the ancient civilization's fate.

Kael said determinedly, "We must uncover the secrets of their downfall to understand the choices we must make in our quest."

With newfound clarity, the companions made a solemn vow to preserve the remnants of the underground civilization and its wisdom. They understood that the echoes carried a timeless message — one that transcended generations and implored them to be the guardians of this sacred knowledge.

As they exited the chamber filled with echoes, the group walked in silence, each member contemplating the significance of what they'd witnessed. Their footsteps echoed through the tunnels, a reminder that they were part of an unbroken chain of connections with the past.

In the depths of the underground world, the companions had experienced a profound resonance with the past. The haunting echoes had revealed a civilization that revered the subterranean realm, living in harmony with its mysteries and wisdom. Yet the echoes also carried a warning—a tragic cataclysm that disrupted the balance between the realms.

Guided by the lessons of history, the group stood united and determined to safeguard the ancient civilization's legacy. Their journey was no longer just about acquiring artifacts but about understanding the underground world's significance and preserving its delicate equilibrium.

As they pressed forward, they embraced their shared destiny and the responsibility that rested on their shoulders. They knew that their choices would shape the future and the legacy they left behind. With the echoes of the past resonating in their hearts, the companions stepped into the next phase of their expedition, ready to face the challenges that lie ahead and embrace the destiny that echoed through the subterranean depths.

4 ❀ The Cavern of Shadows

The group stands at the threshold of the Cavern of Shadows, the entrance engulfed in an eerie mist that sends shivers down their spines. The darkness ahead seems to pulse with ominous energy, challenging their resolve to proceed. As they exchange determined glances, they know that they must face whatever malevolent forces lie within to uncover the answers they seek.

Aiden's voice quivers, "This place feels... unsettling. But we can't turn back now. We must be brave and push forward."

Maya grips her satchel tightly, "Agreed. There might be vital clues within this cavern that could lead us closer to the truth."

The companions take their first steps into the cavern of darkness, the darkness swallowing them whole. The narrow passages twist and turn, making it difficult to discern the way forward. Unease settles upon the companions as they sense a presence lurking in the shadows, watching their every move.

Kael unsheathes his dagger, "I've got a feeling we're not alone. Be on your guard, everyone."

Malevolent forces manifest, and haunting whispers fill the air. Each member of the group confronts their deepest fears and insecurities, battling unsettling illusions that threaten to break their spirit. Yet, as they clasp hands and remind each other of their shared purpose, their courage surges, and they press on together.

Elara's voice remains steady, "These illusions are trying to shake us, but we won't succumb to fear. We are stronger together."

As they delve deeper, flashes of insight emerge from the shadows. The cavern seems to offer fragments of forgotten knowledge, revealing whispers of the enchanted forest's origins and the cataclysm that befell it. The group realizes that the Cavern of Shadows is not just a realm of malevolence, but a realm of revelation, guiding them toward a greater understanding of their purpose.

Gideon observes the mysterious writings on the walls, "These markings might hold the key to understanding what happened in the past. We must decipher them."

The companions' loyalty to one another faces tests as moments of uncertainty arise. They must navigate not only the darkness in the cavern but also the doubts within themselves. Yet, through mutual trust and perseverance, they reaffirm their commitment to the quest.

Maya shares her fears, "I can't help but wonder if I'm fit for this journey if I can truly make a difference."

Kael reassures her, "You're more capable than you think, Maya. We all have our doubts, but together, we balance each other out."

In a pivotal moment of unity, the group uncovers a profound revelation that illuminates the darkness around them. The malevolent forces and unsettling visions were not mere obstacles but catalysts guiding them toward self-discovery and redemption.

Elara uncovers an ancient scroll, "This scroll tells of a time when the balance between the realms was disrupted. It hints at the role we must play in restoring it."

The cavern becomes a metaphorical mirror, reflecting their inner struggles and vulnerabilities. Each member must confront their shadows, recognizing that their strength lies not in denying them, but in embracing and overcoming them.

Aiden opens up about their fears, "I've always felt like an ordinary person, and now I find myself in this extraordinary quest. I fear I might not be worthy."

Gideon places a reassuring hand on Aiden's shoulder, "Aiden, you possess a courage that lies within your heart. It's what brought us all together. Never doubt your worth."

Amongst the shadows, traces of redemption emerge — a chance to heal the wounds of the past and forge a path toward restoring balance in the enchanted forest. As the group nears the heart of the cavern, they find themselves accepting the darkness, understanding its role in shaping their journey and allowing them to emerge stronger and wiser.

Maya reflects on their journey, "The darkness challenged us, but it also revealed our strength. We've grown closer, and we're ready to face whatever comes next."

Finally, as they step out of the Cavern of Shadows, they are greeted by a glimmer of light. The darkness begins to recede, replaced by the radiance of their shared purpose and newfound wisdom. The companions know that their quest is far from over, but they are now better equipped to face the challenges ahead with courage, unity, and the illumination of truth.

Aiden looks back at the cavern's entrance, "The Cavern of Shadows may have tested us, but it also taught us valuable lessons about ourselves and our journey."

The Cavern of Shadows has become a crucible of transformation for the group. In this realm of darkness and malevolence, they have confronted their deepest fears and doubts, emerging stronger and enlightened. The haunting whispers and unsettling illusions have served a greater purpose, guiding them towards a profound understanding of their quest and their inner selves.

Elara smiles, "We faced the darkness, and we emerged stronger and wiser. Our unity is our greatest strength."

5 ✳ The Guardians' Blessing

In this sacred space, the companions stand in awe as the guardians of the underground world reveal its most guarded secrets. Their voices carry the weight of ages past, and each word spoken resonates deep within the hearts of the group.

Maya listens intently, her eyes wide with wonder, "The wisdom they possess is beyond anything I could have imagined. It's like we're witnessing the history of an entire civilization."

Elara nods in agreement, "Their knowledge is a treasure trove of ancient wisdom. We must cherish and protect it."

As the guardians speak, the companions learn about the ancient prophecy that foretells the arrival of individuals from above destined to restore the underground world's balance and safeguard its secrets for the greater good. The realization dawns upon them that they are the fulfilment of this prophecy, chosen for a purpose beyond their understanding.

Aiden gazes at the guardians, "It's a lot to take in, but I feel a profound connection to this place and its history."

Gideon's hand rests on Aiden's shoulder, "We're in this together, Aiden. Trust in our unity and purpose, and we'll prevail."

With the blessings of the guardians, the companions feel a surge of energy — an ethereal blessing bestowed upon them. They sense their abilities enhanced, and their connection to the underground world deepened. It is a tangible manifestation of the guardians' trust and the recognition of their pure intentions.

Kael grins, "I feel like I could take on the world right now! This blessing is extraordinary."

The companions are united by the guardians' wisdom and the shared experience of receiving their blessings. They understand that their quest extends beyond their desires, transcending into a collective responsibility to protect the underground world's legacy.

But the group's journey is not over yet. The guardians present the companions with one final trial—the most challenging of all. It is a test that will put their unity and resolve to the ultimate test, demanding their understanding of the underground world's significance and their unwavering commitment to preserving its secrets.

Elara's eyes sparkle with determination, "This trial will be the ultimate test of our strength and our unity. We must stay true to our purpose."

The trial pushes the companions to their limits, challenging their emotional, mental, and physical fortitude. Yet, through their shared purpose and unyielding determination, they endure. They face moments of doubt and uncertainty, but their bond strengthens with each step, solidified by the wisdom of the guardians.

Maya takes Aiden's hand, "We've come so far together. We can face anything if we support each other."

Finally, after what feels like an eternity of trials, the

companions emerge triumphant. Their unity, courage, and reverence for the underground world's sanctity have proven their worthiness to bear the guardians' blessing and charge.

Kael wipes the sweat from his forehead, "That was no walk in the park, but we did it! Together, we are unstoppable."

In the moment of triumph, a revelation unfolds before them—the underground world's significance goes beyond its mere existence. It is a realm of harmony, balance, and profound wisdom, a place where the connection between the surface and the depths is revered.

Gideon reflects, "The guardians' charge is not just about artifacts and history. It's about protecting the delicate balance that binds our two worlds."

With the knowledge granted by the guardians, the companions come to realize that they are now part of a timeless legacy. Their actions will ripple through generations, shaping the destiny of the underground world and its connection to the surface realm.

Aiden nods, "Our journey is much bigger than ourselves. We hold the responsibility of preserving the underground world for the future."

With a sense of awe and humility, the companions accept the guardians' charge—to protect the underground world's secrets and ensure its delicate balance endures for generations to come. They pledge their unwavering commitment to this sacred responsibility, understanding that they are now not only travellers but guardians themselves.

Elara smiles, "We are now the keepers of this realm's legacy. Let us carry this duty with pride and reverence."

The guardians' blessing and the revelations they have received strengthen the companions' resolve. They carry the wisdom of the ages within them, knowing that they are custodians of a profound legacy. As they step out of the sacred chamber, they are filled with determination and a renewed sense of purpose.

Kael raises his hand, "To the Guardians of the Underground! We will protect this world with all our might!"

Their journey continues, and the companions now understand the true significance of their quest. With the guardians' blessing guiding their path, they venture forth, ready to face whatever challenges lie ahead, knowing that they have been chosen to protect and preserve the magical world that they have come to cherish. Embracing their roles as Guardians of the Underground, the companions walk forward with courage, unity, and a profound reverence for the subterranean realm and its secrets.

6 ❋ Embers of Resilience

In the glow of the torches, the companions gather, taking a moment to reflect on their experiences within the treacherous tunnels.

Maya's eyes shimmer with gratitude, "I never imagined we'd come this far, but together, we've faced every challenge."

Aiden nods, "We've grown so much through this journey, not just as individuals, but as a united force."

Their unexpected allies within the tunnels, the creatures of the underground world, make themselves known once more. They reveal themselves to be the guardians' emissaries — beings who observe the underground world and play a vital role in safeguarding its secrets.

Elara gasps in amazement, "To think these creatures are the guardians' emissaries, watching over this realm all along!"

The emissaries share cryptic messages with the companions, guiding them towards the next phase of their journey. They speak of an ancient artifact — a key that unlocks the core of the underground world's mysteries.

Kael grins, "An artifact of immense importance awaits us! Let's find it and unlock the truths of this realm!"

To find the artifact, the group must traverse through the heart of the underground realm — a path filled with both awe-inspiring wonders and grave dangers.

As the companions continue their expedition, they encounter magnificent underground landscapes. Bioluminescent flora and fauna illuminate their way, revealing the beauty of the underground world. Yet, the allure of the enchanting scenery does not distract them from the awareness that they remain in a realm of secrets and untold power.

Gideon marvels at the sights, "This realm holds wonders beyond imagination. But we must stay focused on our purpose."

In their search for the ancient artifact, they must decipher riddles and solve intricate puzzles left by the guardians. Each challenge draws upon the unique talents of the companions, and they realize that they are stronger as a collective—a harmonious symphony of skills working in unison.

Elara smiles, "Our abilities complement one another perfectly. Together, we can conquer any obstacle."

Through their journey, the companions come across the remnants of an ancient civilization—the first inhabitants of the underground world. Ruins and relics whisper tales of the past, hinting at the civilization's profound reverence for the realm's secrets and the rituals they once performed.

Maya studies the relics, "These artifacts hold the wisdom of a forgotten era. We must learn from their reverence."

As they delve deeper, the group faces trials that test their understanding of the underground world's delicate balance. They must navigate situations where decisions carry weighty consequences, requiring them to consider the long-term effects of their actions.

Aiden looks troubled, "Each choice we make carries consequences beyond ourselves. We must be mindful of our impact."

In moments of doubt, the echoes of the guardians' wisdom guide them. The blessings bestowed upon them serve as a beacon of hope, infusing them with strength and clarity.

Kael nods, "The guardians' blessings remind us of our purpose and grant us the strength to endure."

The companions come to trust their instincts, knowing that their intentions are pure and that they are meant to be guardians of this realm.

Amidst their trials, they encounter challenges that require compromise and collaboration. Their unity and selflessness are put to the test as they grapple with differing perspectives and seek to find common ground.

Elara says thoughtfully, "Our unity is our greatest strength. We must listen to one another and find balance."

In a moment of revelation, the companions come across the ancient artifact—a key that unlocks the core of the underground world's mysteries. As they hold it in their hands, they sense the weight of their responsibility—the guardianship they have been entrusted with.

Gideon's eyes gleam with determination, "This artifact is not just a key. It's a symbol of the trust the guardians have placed in us."

Their journey through the heart of the underground world has honed their resilience, unity, and understanding of the realm's significance. The companions emerge from the cavern of embers stronger and more determined than ever before.

Maya takes a deep breath, "We've faced the trials, and our unity remains unshaken. We're ready for whatever comes next."

They know that their quest is not over yet, and the challenges ahead will test them in ways they cannot yet comprehend. But as they set their sights on the horizon, they embrace the embers of resilience that burn within them.

Kael smiles at his companions, "Together, we'll face the future with courage, for we are the Guardians of the Underground."

With courage, unity, and the unwavering commitment to be the Guardians of the Underground, they are prepared to face whatever lies ahead—to preserve its secrets, protect its balance, and ensure that the magic of this realm endures for generations to come. Their journey continues, fuelled by the embers of resilience that burn brightly within each of them.

7 ❈ The Luminescent Key

As they continue their journey, the companions find themselves drawn deeper into the underground world's heart. The luminescent crystals guide their path, illuminating the way through the ever-changing landscape.

Maya marvels at the mesmerizing sight, "These crystals are like stars in the night sky. They hold so much beauty and wisdom."

Aiden nods, "It's as if they're guiding us, showing us the way to the heart of this realm."

Their interactions with the crystals become more than just an exploration; it feels like a communion with the underground world's essence.

Elara reflects, "The crystals seem to resonate with us, as if they understand our purpose here."

Kael grins, "I have a feeling they know we're the ones destined to protect this realm."

The luminescent key remains a source of wonder and intrigue. As they encounter obstacles along their path, the artifact reacts to specific crystals, opening hidden passages and revealing concealed truths.

Gideon observes, "The key is attuned to the crystals' energy. It's like a magical bridge between us and the underground world."

Their unity and resourcefulness are tested as they face challenges that require quick thinking and decisive action.

Aiden calls out, "Quick, the crystal over there! Use the key to activate the mechanism!"

With each trial, their bond grows stronger, and they rely on one another's strengths to overcome obstacles.

Maya smiles, "Together, we're unstoppable. Our unity is our greatest asset."

As they journey deeper into the underground world, echoes of the ancient civilization become more prevalent. Carvings and inscriptions on the walls depict rituals and ceremonies performed in honour of the luminescent crystals.

Elara studies the inscriptions, "These carvings show how much these crystals were revered by the ancients."

The group finds themselves drawn to the rituals, as if guided by the echoes of the past.

Kael muses, "There's something sacred about these rituals. They remind us of the bond between the realms."

As they progress, the companions come to understand that the luminescent crystals are more than just decorative; they are conduits of energy, representing the life force that sustains the underground world's magic.

Gideon reflects, "The crystals are the heart of this realm— the source of its magic and harmony."

Their understanding of the underground world deepens, and they begin to see it not as a separate realm but as an interconnected part of their own reality.

Aiden muses, "The surface and the underground world are intertwined, like two sides of the same coin."

In the heart of the underground world, they face their most significant challenge — the luminescent key unlocks a hidden chamber housing ancient tomes and artifacts that unveil the realm's history.

Elara's eyes widen, "These tomes hold the secrets of generations past. The knowledge is profound."

The revelations in the hidden chamber strengthen their resolve. They know they are now entrusted with a sacred duty — to protect the underground world's secrets and preserve its luminescent wonders.

Kael declares, "We are the guardians, the stewards of this realm. Its magic is in our hands."

The luminescent key becomes more than just a physical artifact; it embodies the companions' shared purpose.

Maya adds, "The key reminds us of why we're here — to safeguard this realm and its delicate balance."

As they step out of the hidden chamber, the companions are filled with determination and reverence.

Gideon says solemnly, "We carry the knowledge of the underground world within us now. We must proceed with utmost care."

The luminescent wonders have left an indelible mark on their hearts and minds, reminding them of the interconnectedness of all things.

Elara reflects, "The beauty of this realm lies not just in its physical wonders but in the harmony it represents."

With each step, the companions grow more resilient, unified, and attuned to the realm's magic.

Aiden smiles, "We're more than just travellers; we're Guardians of the Underground — protectors of its magic."

As they proceed, the luminescent key remains a beacon of hope—a reminder of the wonders they have encountered and the profound responsibility they bear.

Kael concludes, "We carry the luminescent key with pride, for we are entrusted with the magic of this realm."

With courage and determination, the companions continue their journey as Guardians of the Underground, ready to face whatever lies ahead with unity and the unwavering commitment to protect and preserve the luminescent wonders of this ancient realm. Their quest is far from over, but they step forward with hearts ablaze, guided by the luminescent key and the profound knowledge they carry within.

8 ❀ Bonds Forged in The Labyrinth

As the companions venture deeper into the labyrinth, echoes of their laughter and shared camaraderie resonate in their thoughts, a reminder of the unity they once had. However, the labyrinth's disorienting twists and turns have put their bonds to the test, leaving them feeling uncertain and vulnerable.

Aiden, trying to keep his spirits up, says, "We'll find our way back to each other. We've faced challenges before and always come out stronger."

Elara nods, though worry is evident in her eyes. "You're right, Aiden. We can't lose hope. We must trust that our bond will guide us back together."

The labyrinth is teeming with mysterious creatures native to the underground world. Some of these creatures prove to be helpful guides, showing the companions the way forward.

Maya smiles gratefully at one of the creatures, "Thank you for leading us. We're grateful for your help."

Others, however, present unexpected challenges, testing the companions' empathy and resourcefulness.

Kael cautiously approaches a creature blocking their path. "Easy now. We don't want any trouble."

The creature's demeanour softens, and it steps aside, allowing the group to pass. They realize that understanding and compassion are crucial in this realm.

As they journey through the labyrinth, the companions find themselves confronting their personal fears and insecurities. The darkness becomes a canvas for their inner demons to surface.

Gideon clenches his fists, trying to quell his anxieties. "I'm supposed to be the strong one, but I'm scared. Scared of losing you all."

Elara places a comforting hand on his shoulder, "Gideon, being scared doesn't make you weak. We all have our fears, and that's what makes us human. We're in this together."

The labyrinth becomes a crucible for self-discovery and growth. The companions realize that they are not defined solely by their roles within the group but by the unique qualities they bring to the collective whole.

Maya, using her archaeologist skills, deciphers a hidden message. "This inscription speaks of individuality and unity working hand in hand. It's like we're meant to embrace our differences and come together as one."

The challenges in the labyrinth require quick thinking and collaboration. The companions must rely on each other's strengths to overcome the obstacles.

Kael calls out to the others, "We need to work as a team, trust each other, and communicate. Only then can we navigate this labyrinth safely."

They leave messages of encouragement and hope for one another, reaffirming their shared purpose and determination to reunite.

Aiden writes, "I know we'll find each other again. Our bond is stronger than any maze."

Their voices echo through the labyrinth, a testament to their unwavering connection as Guardians of the Underground.

As they continue their journey, the companions encounter cryptic symbols and markings in the labyrinth, hinting at the realm's deeper mysteries.

Elara observes, "These symbols are like pieces of a puzzle. They must hold the key to something greater."

The labyrinth pushes them to their limits, but they persevere. Each near-miss and narrow escape brings them closer to reuniting.

Maya breathes a sigh of relief as they find each other, "We did it! We're together again."

The reunion fills their hearts with joy, and they share warm embraces, knowing that their unity has withstood the labyrinth's trials.

Gideon grins, "We're stronger together. No maze can break our bond."

With their bonds forged in the labyrinth's darkness, the companions emerge with a renewed sense of purpose and unity.

Aiden declares, "We've faced the labyrinth and come out stronger. Nothing can stop us now."

Maya adds, "Our journey continues, but our bond remains steadfast. We are Guardians of the Underground—protectors of its secrets and its luminescent wonders."

As they step forward, hearts ablaze with determination, the companions walk united and ready to face whatever lies ahead. Their journey has melted them into a cohesive force, prepared to preserve the realm's magic and uncover its ancient knowledge. The labyrinth has not weakened them but strengthened their resolve to be the Guardians of the Underground, dedicated to preserving the realm's secrets, safeguarding its luminescent wonders, and ensuring that the harmony between the surface and the depths endures for generations to come.

9 ❁ Embers of Redemption

The companions gather around a small campfire, the soft glow of the embers mirroring the determination in their eyes. The ancient prophecies they discovered have deeply resonated within their souls, shaping their newfound purpose as Guardians of the Underground.

Elara speaks, her voice filled with conviction, "We are chosen to protect this realm and its luminescent wonders. But now, we also understand that redemption lies in acknowledging the darkness we encountered and seeking healing for the wounds of the past."

Aiden nods, "The heart of darkness wasn't just a malevolent force. It was a reflection of the realm's history and unresolved grievances. We need to confront the past to bring balance and redemption."

The group agrees to delve deeper into the underground world's history, seeking records, artifacts, and insights that shed light on the ancient civilization and the entity's origins. They know that understanding the past is key to breaking the cycle of darkness.

As they explore further, they encounter echoes of the ancient civilization—whispers of lost heroes and forgotten wisdom. These tales inspire them, guiding their path towards redemption and reconciliation.

Maya uncovers a mural depicting a long-lost hero's sacrifice. "This hero gave everything to protect the realm. We must learn from their courage and selflessness."

Kael adds, "We must also learn from their mistakes. The past can't be erased, but we can learn and grow from it."

The luminescent key continues to unlock hidden chambers, revealing fragments of the past. Each discovery brings them closer to the heart of the underground world's history and the keys to redemption.

Gideon looks at the key in his hand, "This artifact is more than just a physical key. It's unlocking the secrets of our journey, guiding us towards redemption." As they seek to understand the ancient civilization, the group faces their own inner turmoil. The weight of their responsibility as guardians weighs heavily on them.

Elara confides, "I worry that we might not be enough to fulfil our duty. What if we fail?"

Aiden reassures her, "We're not alone in this. We have each other, and that's what makes us strong. We'll face the challenges together."

Along their journey, the companions encounter the last guardians who remained faithful to their duty. These ancient beings impart wisdom, reminding them of the significance of their role. An ancient guardian speaks, "You carry the embers of redemption within you. Let them guide you towards a future of harmony."

As they delve into the underground world's history, the group begins to understand that darkness is an integral force in the universe — a part of the delicate balance that shapes life's intricacies.

Maya observes, "The realm's past is a reflection of its present. We must embrace darkness and light to find true harmony."

The companions seek to forge a new path for the underground world, one that honours the realm's history while fostering a legacy of compassion and understanding. Kael says, "The cycle of darkness can end with us. We have the power to change the future."

With each step forward, the embers of redemption burn brighter within the companions. They become the custodians of the underground world's history, ensuring that the past serves as a guiding light rather than a shadow.

Gideon declares, "We won't let darkness define the underground world. We will be the ones to shape its legacy."

Their journey as Guardians of the Underground continues, guided by the embers of redemption within them. They know that true redemption lies in preserving the realm's balance, protecting its luminescent wonders, and forging a future that harmonizes darkness and light. Elara looks at her companions, "Our journey is far from over, but we have each other and the embers of redemption to light our way."

The companions stand united, their determination unwavering. They are Guardians of the Underground, ready to face the future with compassion, resilience, and a profound understanding of the realm's delicate balance. With the embers of redemption leading their way, they are prepared to ensure that the underground world thrives in harmony for generations to come.

10 ❀ Whispers of the Forgotten

The adventurers make their way through the dark passageways, following the faint echoes that lead them deeper into the hidden enclave. A soft symphony of whispers fills the air, as if the very walls were alive with the tales of the past.

Elara listens intently, "Do you hear that? It's like the voices of the ancient guardians are guiding us."

Aiden nods, "These whispers must hold the key to the realm's deepest mysteries. We must tread carefully."

As they proceed, the group encounters ancient inscriptions etched into the walls. Kael runs his fingers over the markings, trying to decipher their meaning.

"These inscriptions speak of a prophecy—a prophecy that tells of our arrival," Kael announces.

Maya adds, "It seems that we were destined to be here, to continue the legacy of the ancient guardians."

The revelations within the enclave intertwine with the tales they heard from the artifact's guardians. The pieces of history fall into place, connecting the dots of the underground world's past.

Gideon observes, "The whispers and the guardians' tales—everything is connected. We are part of a grand tapestry of history."

As they delve deeper, the group finds relics that offer glimpses into the realm's origin and the civilizations that once thrived within its embrace.

"These relics are like windows to the past," Elara marvels. "They hold the knowledge of ages."

The companions learn ancient teachings that have been lost to time. The wisdom of the past becomes a guiding light, helping them navigate the complexities of their role as Guardians of the Underground.

Aiden reflects, "The past teaches us the consequences of discord and the value of harmony. We must learn from it to protect the realm."

The echoes recount tales of ancient conflicts and betrayals that scarred the underground world. The adventurers face the remnants of old wounds that have yet to heal, realizing the importance of understanding the realm's history to protect its future.

Kael says, "The past mistakes have consequences that echo through time. We must not repeat them."

In the enclave, the group discovers the artifact's original purpose and its role in safeguarding the underground world. They understand that they are not just wielders of power but also the keepers of a legacy.

Maya says, "The relic's purpose goes beyond the physical—it's about preserving the realm's delicate balance and the wisdom of the ancient guardians."

However, not all within the enclave is benign. Malevolent forces seek to exploit the whispers' power for their dark purposes.

Elara clenches her fists, "We can't let the darkness take hold. We must confront it."

The group faces a profound choice—to seek redemption for the malevolent entities or to vanquish them. They draw upon the wisdom of the past to find a harmonious resolution.

Gideon adds, "Darkness can be redeemed, but it requires the willingness to embrace the light within."

Through an act of empathy and compassion, the adventurers find a way to heal the malevolent forces and restore balance to the underground world.

Kael says, "Redemption is not about erasing darkness, but about finding harmony within it."

As they depart from the enclave, the whispers fade, leaving a lingering sense of enlightenment within the group.

Maya smiles, "The whispers may be gone, but their wisdom remains with us."

With the relic's power and the echoes of the past in their hands, the companions emerge transformed.

Elara declares, "We are now the guardians of ancient knowledge, tasked with protecting the realm's harmony for all eternity."

As they continue their quest, guided by the whispers of the forgotten, the adventurers are filled with a sense of purpose and unity.

Aiden says, "We carry the legacy of the ancient guardians within us. Our journey is interwoven with the realm's enduring history."

The adventurers know that their quest as Guardians of the Underground is far from over, but they are now equipped with the wisdom of the past and the power of the relic.

Gideon concludes, "The echoes of the past will continue to guide us, reminding us of our shared purpose and the promise of a harmonious future."

With their hearts full of determination and reverence for the realm's mysteries, the companions walk forward, ready to protect the underground world's delicate balance and preserve its luminescent wonders for generations to come. Their journey continues, guided by the enigmatic whispers of the forgotten—an eternal symphony that binds the surface and the depths in harmony.

11 ❂ The Symphony of Elements

In the wake of the subterranean storm, the adventurers find themselves seeking refuge in a vast cavern nestled deep within the underground world. The howling winds and torrential rain make it impossible to continue their journey, forcing them to take shelter and wait for the storm to pass.

Elara raises her voice above the roaring storm, "We need to find a safe place to wait out this tempest. The elemental forces are fierce, and it's too dangerous to continue."

Gideon scans their surroundings, his eyes catching sight of a cavern entrance partially concealed by cascading waterfalls. "Over there! That cavern looks promising. It should provide enough shelter until the storm subsides."

The group quickly hurries toward the cavern, rain soaking their clothes and boots. Once inside, they find themselves surrounded by a natural amphitheatre of sorts, with stalactites and stalagmites forming an awe-inspiring display.

Maya shivers slightly, "At least we're safe from the storm in here. But I've never experienced such an intense subterranean tempest before."

Aiden nods in agreement, "It's as if the elements themselves are raging. But I can't help but feel that there's something significant about this storm."

Kael gazes at the cavern's entrance, where the storm's fury is evident. "Perhaps the storm is a manifestation of the underground world's magic—a symphony of elements reacting to some unknown force."

The adventurers huddle together to preserve warmth, their minds filled with curiosity and concern. As the storm rages outside, they share stories of their encounters with elemental beings and reflect on the lessons they learned.

The adventurers walk in awe as they witness the underground world's transformation after the subterranean storm. The realm is a symphony of elements—an intricate dance of earth, water, fire, and air in harmonious balance.

Elara breathes in the refreshing air, "Nature's power has breathed new life into this place. It's incredible to see how the underground world can recover after such a storm."

Gideon nods, "The realm's resilience is a testament to its enduring magic. It's as if the symphony of elements is orchestrating its regeneration."

As they explore further, the group encounters areas where nature has begun to reclaim what the storm disrupted. Delicate sprouts of new growth emerge from the damp soil, and vibrant plant life paints the chambers in shades of green.

Maya smiles, "The underground world is healing itself, guided by the symphony of elements. It's a beautiful process."

Kael adds, "It reminds us that the symphony of elements isn't just about forces of destruction and creation—it's also about renewal and restoration."

During their journey, the adventurers come across elemental beings they encountered during the storm. The once-enigmatic creatures now seem more approachable, and the group understands that they are embodiments of the realm's elemental balance.

Aiden observes, "These elemental beings represent the essence of the underground world's magic—the very heart of the symphony of elements."

The group resolves to find the elemental nexus—the heart of the underground world's elemental balance. They believe that within this nexus lies the key to preserving the realm's harmony and safeguarding its delicate dance of elements.

Elara says, "The elemental nexus holds the essence of the underground world's magic. It's where we must go to fulfil our purpose as Guardians."

Guided by the teachings of the ancient guardians, the adventurers face trials that test their connection to the elements. Each trial becomes a mirror of the self—an opportunity for introspection and growth.

Gideon reflects, "These trials challenge us to understand and respect the elemental forces that sustain the underground world."

In the elemental nexus, the adventurers confront challenges that reflect their inner struggles and relationship with the elements. Each member must demonstrate their understanding and connection to the elemental forces.

Maya realizes, "Our unity as a group depends on how well we harmonize our individual connections to the elements."

In a profound ceremony, the elemental guardians bless the adventurers, acknowledging them as the chosen protectors of the underground world's balance.

Kael looks on in reverence, "The symphony of elements recognizes our bond with the realm. It's an honour to be chosen."

Each adventurer receives a unique gift—a token of elemental wisdom that enhances their abilities and serves as a reminder of their purpose.

Aiden holds the gift in his hand, "This token symbolizes our newfound connection to the elements. We carry the wisdom of the symphony within us."

As the group departs from the elemental nexus, they carry with them the symphony of elements—the knowledge, the bond, and the wisdom that will guide them in their continued quest.

Elara says, "The symphony of elements resonates within our souls. It will guide us as we protect the underground world's magic."

Gideon adds, "Our journey is about celebrating the majesty of the realm—the wondrous harmony of the symphony."

With the symphony of elements in their hearts, the adventurers embrace their roles as Guardians of the Underground. Their quest is not just to preserve the realm's magic but also to celebrate its beauty.

Maya says, "We are the custodians of life's enchanting dance—the symphony that exists at the intersection of darkness and light."

The adventurers set their sights on the future, ready to protect the realm's harmony for all time.

Kael declares, "With the symphony of elements as our guide, we walk this path together as Guardians of the Underground."

As they step into the unknown, the symphony of elements plays within their hearts—a symphony of unity, balance, and enduring magic. Their quest is not solitary, but a collective endeavour—one that weaves the tapestry of life's enchanting dance. With the symphony of elements as their guiding melody, the adventurers embrace their destiny, ready to protect the underground world's harmony for generations to come.

12 ❧ Threads of Destiny

The adventurers venture further into the underground world, guided by fragments of forgotten tales provided by the enigmatic wanderer. The figure draped in ancient wisdom leads them to hidden chambers, where they unearth long-lost artifacts and gain insight into the realm's origins.

As they stand in awe before an ancient relic, Elara asks the wanderer, "Who were the guardians of these artifacts? And what is their connection to the underground world's balance?"

The wanderer's eyes hold a glimmer of ancient knowledge as he responds, "The guardians were once chosen protectors, like you. They were entrusted with preserving the underground world's magic and maintaining its delicate harmony."

Gideon contemplates, "So, our quest to protect the realm's balance is intertwined with the legacy of these ancient guardians."

The wanderer nods, "Indeed, the threads of destiny bind you to their purpose. You are Guardians of the Underground, carrying forward their legacy."

Among their fateful encounters is a guardian—an ancient being with the responsibility of safeguarding forbidden knowledge. The group must prove their noble intentions to gain access to this guarded wisdom.

As they face the guardian, Maya speaks with determination, "We seek knowledge not for personal gain but to preserve the realm's magic and protect its balance."

The guardian studies them intently, "To wield such power comes with great responsibility. Are you prepared to bear the consequences of this knowledge?"

Kael hesitates, knowing the allure of power, "It's a tempting offer, but our duty as Guardians must guide us."

The guardian nods approvingly, "You have shown wisdom in your choice. The forbidden knowledge remains safe within these chambers."

Their decision to resist temptation reaffirms their commitment as Guardians of the Underground, but the journey ahead is not without its perils.

In their pursuit of answers, the adventurers encounter an ethereal oracle—an enigmatic figure gifted with foresight.

The oracle speaks in riddles, "The threads of destiny are woven in intricate patterns. Choices you make will alter the tapestry of fate."

Aiden seeks clarity, "What do these visions foretell? And how do we ensure our choices shape a positive future?"

The oracle's response is cryptic, "Seek the harmony between heart and mind. Trust in your connection to the underground world's magic."

Their encounters with enigmatic beings provide vital insights, but they also warn of impending perils and moral dilemmas. The group must interpret these visions and make choices that shape their path.

As they venture deeper, the adventurers find themselves entangled in a complex web of allegiances. Some prove to be unlikely allies, while others harbour hidden motives.

Elara reflects, "Our quest has far-reaching consequences, and we must tread carefully in forming alliances."

Gideon agrees, "The underground world's magic is delicate, and we must guard against those who may seek to exploit it."

In their journey, they encounter a rival group—another band of seekers vying for the same secrets and artifacts.

Maya voices concern, "Our rival group poses a significant challenge. We must stay focused and true to our purpose."

Kael adds, "Our dedication as Guardians must outweigh their pursuit of personal gain."

The rivalry escalates, and one of the group members succumbs to temptation, betraying the companions.

Aiden confronts the betrayer, "Your actions have endangered us all. How could you betray the trust we placed in you?"

The betrayer's voice trembles with regret, "I was consumed by the allure of power. But now I see the grave mistake I made."

The group faces the challenge of reconciliation and redemption. The path to redemption becomes a transformative journey for the betrayer.

Elara asserts, "Redemption is possible when one confronts their mistakes and seeks to right their wrongs."

In search of counsel, the adventurers seek an ancient council of wise beings who have guarded the underground world for eons.

The council imparts ancient wisdom, revealing the implications of their quest on the realm's destiny.

Gideon listens intently, "Our actions ripple through the tapestry of fate, impacting the underground world's past and shaping its future."

Their encounters and decisions are woven into the fabric of their destinies. The adventurers realize that their journey is about embracing the complexity of the realm they are bound to protect.

Maya says with conviction, "Our choices hold immense significance. We must remain true to our purpose and protect the underground world's magic."

Kael adds, "The threads of destiny intertwine us with the realm's fate. We carry the burden of our responsibility as true Guardians."

As they journey forth, the underground world's mysteries deepen, and the tapestry of fate continues to unfurl.

Elara declares, "Our quest is not just about unravelling enigmas but also about embracing the profound connection we share with the realm's magic."

The group stands united, drawing strength from one another and the wisdom of their fateful encounters.

Aiden speaks with determination, "Together, we will safeguard the underground world's magic and preserve its delicate harmony."

As the threads of destiny intertwine, the adventurers embrace their roles as Guardians of the Underground. Their quest is not solitary, but a collective endeavour—one that weaves the tapestry of life's intricate dance.

Maya concludes, "In the symphony of elements and the enigmatic encounters we face, we find purpose, unity, and the enduring magic of the underground world."

With their hearts entwined with the threads of destiny, the adventurers step into the unknown, ready to protect the underground world's harmony for generations to come. Their journey is one of profound significance, carrying the essence of the realm's magic within their souls—the luminescent wonders they are sworn to safeguard for all eternity.

13 ❀ Embrace of Destiny

As the adventurers approach the Crystal Core's sanctum, they are greeted by the guardians who have stood watch over this hallowed ground for eons. These enigmatic beings, wise and ancient, test the adventurers' understanding of the realm's magic and the unity that binds them as a group.

Guardian of the Crystal Core: "Welcome, Guardians of the Underground. You have journeyed far, and now you stand at the heart of our realm's magic. The trials you face here will challenge not only your skills but also your commitment to preserving the delicate balance."

Maya: "We are honoured to be here. Our purpose as Guardians is unwavering, and we seek to protect the underground world's magic with all our hearts."

The Crystal Core's sanctum is a sight to behold — a place of radiant glow and shimmering crystals. As the adventurers step inside, visions of the underground world's history unfold before their eyes, revealing the rise and fall of civilizations, the wisdom of ancient guardians, and the ebb and flow of the realm's magic over countless generations.

Elara: "These visions are breathtaking. It's as if the realm's entire history is speaking to us."

Aiden: "The prophecies we once struggled to understand now align, guiding our quest."

The Crystal Core reveals the duality of its power — an intricate balance between creation and destruction.

Gideon: "The magic of the underground world is neither wholly good nor evil. It's a force that can be harnessed for either purpose."

Kael: "As true guardians, it's our responsibility to ensure that the realm's magic remains a force of harmony and hope."

Within the Crystal Core, the adventurers confront their inner struggles and desires.

Maya: "This place is a crucible of self-discovery. We must face our vulnerabilities to embrace our roles fully."

Elara: "We stand together, supporting each other in this journey of growth."

As the trials continue, the adventurers find strength in their unity and the Crystalline Covenant bestowed upon them by the guardians.

Guardian of the Crystal Core: "The Crystalline Covenant binds you together as a group — one that understands the significance of its quest."

Kael: "We embrace this responsibility, knowing the underground world's destiny is in our hands."

With each trial overcome, the adventurers emerge from the Crystal Core transformed, carrying the legacy of their quest.

Gideon: "The weight of our purpose feels both awe-inspiring and humbling."

Aiden: "The realm's magic courses through us, and we are now true Guardians of the Underground."

The adventurers bid farewell to the guardians and the ancient place of revelation, stepping back into the world aboveground.

Maya: "Our return marks the beginning of a new chapter. Our journey has only just begun."

Elara: "We walk forward with determination and hope, knowing we are the chosen protectors of the underground world's destiny."

United in their commitment to preserve the realm's magic, the adventurers stand ready to confront any challenges that lie ahead.

Kael: "Our bond is unbreakable, and we face the future together."

Aiden: "We are the guardians of hope and harmony, ready to embrace our profound and noble destiny."

With the essence of the Crystal Core in their hearts, the adventurers step into the world, their purpose clear and their resolve unshaken.

Guardian of the Crystal Core: "May the underground world's magic guide and protect you always. Go forth, Guardians of the Underground, and weave the threads of destiny with courage and wisdom."

Maya: "We will uphold our oath and safeguard the underground world's luminescent wonders for eternity."

As they venture forth, the adventurers carry the essence of the Crystal Core — the heart of the underground world's magic — within their souls. Their journey is a testament to their commitment, unity, and the enduring bond they share with the realm they are sworn to protect.

With hearts aligned with the realm's destiny, they step into the unknown, ready to embrace the profound and noble destiny that awaits them as true Guardians of the Underground.

14 ❁ Redemption's Embrace

As emotions run high and accusations fly, the group faces a moment of self-reflection. Each adventurer is compelled to confront their own vulnerabilities and biases, acknowledging that everyone carries their burdens and imperfections.

Kael: "I never thought this would happen. How could they betray us like this?"

Elara: "We must remember that everyone has their struggles. We are not immune to mistakes either."

Gideon: "But this betrayal shakes the very foundation of our trust. Can we ever forgive and trust them again?"

Seeking resolution, some members of the group advocate for forgiveness and redemption.

Aiden: "Understanding their motivations is crucial before we decide their fate."

Maya: "Perhaps they deserve a chance at redemption if they genuinely regret their actions."

However, others find it challenging to reconcile their feelings of anger and betrayal, questioning whether trust can ever be restored.

Kael: "I don't know if I can ever trust them again."

Elara: "Betrayal cuts deep, but we must be open to the possibility of healing."

In the midst of this turmoil, a ray of hope emerges—a shared memory or a moment of camaraderie that reminds the adventurers of the bond they once shared.

Gideon: "Remember when we faced the elemental beings together? We were a true team back then."

Maya: "That memory reminds us of what we've overcome together. We can find strength in that."

This glimmer of hope reignites the possibility of reconciliation and rebuilding trust. The journey to redemption becomes a pivotal theme as the group contemplates the path that lies ahead.

The betrayer is offered a chance at redemption, an opportunity to demonstrate remorse and make amends.

Betrayer: "I never meant for things to turn out this way. I was lost and made a terrible mistake."

Elara: "We must tread cautiously, but we should consider the possibility of redemption."

The road to redemption is fraught with challenges, as they must prove their commitment to the group's cause and regain the trust they once held. It is a test of character and perseverance that demands self-reflection and growth.

Aiden: "Redemption requires genuine effort and change. It's not an easy path."

Maya: "If they are truly remorseful, we owe it to ourselves and the realm to give them a chance."

The group engages in open and honest conversations, baring their vulnerabilities and fears, and working towards understanding and forgiveness.

Kael: "I felt betrayed and hurt, but I also see the struggle they went through."

Gideon: "We all have flaws, and it takes courage to admit them."

These heartfelt exchanges become the foundation for healing and rebuilding the trust that was lost.

Elara: "I can't say I trust them completely, but I'm willing to try."

Aiden: "Forgiveness doesn't mean forgetting, but it means giving a chance for growth and change."

The process is arduous, but it strengthens their bond and reaffirms their shared purpose as Guardians of the Underground.

Maya: "We are stronger together. Our bond can withstand this if we choose to embrace redemption."

As they face a new threat in the underground world, one that jeopardizes not only their mission but also the realm's delicate balance, the adventurers realize that their strength lies in their unity.

Gideon: "We may have our differences, but we must stay united to protect the underground world."

They understand that the experience of betrayal has transformed them, making their bond stronger and more resilient.

Kael: "Our journey through betrayal has made us stronger. We must stand together."

In the face of this greater peril, the adventurers confront the betrayer's decision.

Betrayer: "I want to change. I want to prove myself worthy of being a Guardian."

The betrayer must make a momentous choice—to embrace their path to redemption and continue as a true Guardian of the Underground or to succumb to their past actions and walk away from the group forever.

Elara: "This decision will shape their destiny. It's not an easy one to make."

The decision is wrought with inner turmoil and profound significance.

Maya: "We must support them, no matter what they choose."

It tests the betrayer's resolve and commitment to change, offering a chance for true growth and renewal.

Gideon: "Redemption is a journey, not a destination. We must give them the opportunity to grow."

With their resolve renewed and a sense of unity restored, the adventurers march forward into the abyss.

Aiden: "Together, we face whatever challenges await us."

The scars of the past remain, but they now carry a newfound sense of purpose and camaraderie.

Kael: "We may be scarred, but those scars remind us of our strength and resilience."

Together, they are an unbreakable front, ready to face the unknown and protect the underground world's magic with unwavering determination.

Elara: "We may face challenges, but we'll overcome them together."

The journey through betrayal has forged a path towards redemption — an embrace of growth and forgiveness that has deepened their understanding of themselves and one another.

Gideon: "Our journey through betrayal has taught us valuable lessons about compassion and understanding."

As the underground world's protectors, they have emerged stronger, bound by the threads of their shared experiences, and ready to face the challenges that await them.

Maya: "We have grown and changed, and that's what matters now."

In the embrace of redemption, they find the strength to confront the abyss with courage and hope.

Kael: "Our path may be uncertain, but we'll face it together."

With hearts aligned with the realm's destiny, they step into the unknown, ready to embrace the profound and noble destiny that awaits them as true Guardians of the Underground.

15 ❋ The Resonance of Light

Now, as they stand on the precipice of their escape, the adventurers are forever changed by their extraordinary journey. The subterranean world has imprinted its mark upon each of them, and the trials they faced have honed their skills and solidified their unity.

Aiden: "I can hardly believe how much we've grown through this journey."

Maya: "Indeed, the challenges have shaped us into the Guardians we are today."

The bond they share as companions is unbreakable, woven together through moments of triumph and hardship.

Gideon: "We've faced so much together. Our bond is stronger than ever."

Elara: "And it will carry us through whatever lies ahead."

As they emerge from the depths, they carry with them the wisdom of the underground world — the secrets unearthed, the enigmas unravelled, and the lessons learned.

Kael: "The underground world's magic will forever resonate within us."

Elara: "We have unlocked its secrets, and it will guide our steps in the surface world."

The path they have treaded has moulded them into true Guardians of the Underground, protectors of its delicate balance and preservers of its luminescent wonders.

Maya: "We carry the responsibility of preserving its harmony."

Aiden: "And safeguarding its magic for generations to come."

Their escape is a testament to their resilience and dedication. It is not just an ascent from the depths but an ascension to a new sense of purpose and understanding.

Gideon: "We've faced so many challenges, but we've overcome them all."

Kael: "We now know the importance of our quest and the impact we can make."

The underground world's magic will forever resonate within them, guiding their steps as they return to the surface world.

Elara: "As we step back into the light, we'll carry the underground world's essence with us."

Maya: "Its luminescence will shine through us, guiding our way."

As they step back into the light, their hearts are filled with a profound gratitude for the journey they undertook together.

Kael: "I'm grateful for all the moments we shared — both the joys and the struggles."

Aiden: "Those experiences have made us who we are."

They know that their quest is not truly over — it is the beginning of a new chapter, where they will carry the legacy of their adventures and the weight of their responsibilities with courage and conviction.

Gideon: "Our journey is ongoing. The underground world still needs us."

Maya: "And we'll face whatever challenges come our way."

The adventurers ascend from the depths, forever changed, and united in their commitment to preserve the underground world's magic.

Kael: "Our journey has moulded us into Guardians, protectors of the realm's delicate balance."

Elara: "And we'll carry out this duty with unwavering determination."

Their extraordinary journey has moulded them into Guardians, and they embrace this newfound role with determination and hope, ready to face whatever challenges lie ahead.

Aiden: "We've grown so much, but there's still more to learn."

Maya: "And more to protect."

The subterranean world's secrets have left an indelible mark on their souls, and they emerge as beacons of light in the darkness, forever bound by the luminescent wonders they sought to protect.

Gideon: "The underground world's magic is now a part of us."

Elara: "Its luminescence will guide our actions and decisions."

As true Guardians of the Underground, their journey has only just begun. They step forward, their hearts resonating with the realm's magic, their bond unbreakable, and their purpose unwavering. The surface world awaits, and they carry the light of the underground with them, ready to protect its harmony and luminescent wonders for all eternity. The resonance of light shines brightly within them, illuminating their path as they embrace the destiny, they were destined to fulfil.

THE END

What is Sudoku?

A puzzle in which missing numbers are to be filled into a 9 by 9 grid of squares which are subdivided into 3 by 3 boxes so that every row, every column, and every box contains the numbers 1 through 9.

Sudoku Rule No. - 1: Use Numbers 1-9

Sudoku is played on a grid of 9 x 9 spaces. Within the rows and columns are 9 "squares" (made up of 3 x 3 spaces). Each row, column and square (9 spaces each) needs to be filled out with the numbers 1-9, without repeating any numbers within the row, column or square. Does it sound complicated? As you can see from the image below of an actual Sudoku grid, each Sudoku grid comes with a few spaces already filled in; the more spaces filled in, the easier the game – the more difficult Sudoku puzzles have very few spaces that are already filled in.

Sudoku Rule No. - 2: Don't Repeat Any Numbers.

As you can see, in the upper left square (circled in blue), this square already has 7 out of the 9 spaces filled in. The only numbers missing from the square are 5 and 6. By seeing which numbers are missing from each square, row, or column, we can use process of elimination and deductive reasoning to decide which numbers need to go in each blank space.

For example, in the upper left square, we know we need to add a 5 and a 6 to be able to complete the square, but based on the neighboring rows and squares we cannot clearly deduce which number to add in which space. This means that we should ignore the upper left square for now, and try to fill in spaces in some other areas of the grid instead.

	7	2			4	9		
3		4		8	9	1		
8	1	9			6	2	5	4
7		1					9	5
9					2		7	
			8		7		1	2
4		5			1	6	2	
2	3	7				5		1
				2	5	7		

Sudoku is a game of logic and reasoning, so you shouldn't have to guess. If you don't know what number to put in a certain space, keep scanning the other areas of the grid until you seen an opportunity to place a number. But don't try to "force" anything – Sudoku rewards patience, insights, and recognition of patterns, not blind luck or guessing.

What do we mean by using "process of elimination" to play Sudoku? Here is an example. In this Sudoku grid (shown below), the far left-hand vertical column (circled in Blue) is missing only a few numbers: 1, 5 and 6.

One way to figure out which numbers can go in each space is to use "process of elimination" by checking to see which other numbers are already included within each square – since there can be no duplication of numbers 1-9 within each square (or row or column).

(Cont. on next page)

In this case, we can quickly notice that there are already number 1s in the top left and center-left squares of the grid (with number 1s circled in red). This means that there is only one space remaining in the far-left column where a 1 could possibly go – circled in green. This is how the process of elimination works in Sudoku – you find out which spaces are available, which numbers are missing – and then deduce, based on the position of those numbers within the grid, which numbers fit into each space.

Sudoku rules are relatively uncomplicated – but the game is infinitely varied, with millions of possible number combinations and a wide range of levels of difficulty. But it's all based on the simple principles of using numbers 1-9, filling in the blank spaces based on deductive reasoning, and never repeating any numbers within each square, row, or column.

	7	2				4	9	
3		4		8	9	1		
8	(1)	9			6	2	5	4
7		(1)					9	5
9					2		7	
			8		7		1	2
4		5			1	6	2	
2	3	7				5		1
				2	5	7		

Scan the code and start the video.
How to play Sudoku? (English Language)

Scan the code and start the video.
How to play Sudoku? (Hindi Language)

E-1

7	2	3				1	5	9
6			3		2			8
8				1				2
	7		6	5	4		2	
		4	2		7	3		
	5		9	3	1		4	
5				7				3
4			1		3			6
9	3	2				7	1	4

E-2

		7	1	5		9		
		9	4	3				
5					2		1	3
		6	5		4		2	9
4	3			8			5	7
9	7		3		1	4		
7	6		2					5
				9	6	2		
		3		4	5	6		

1								9
	4		2	6	1		3	
	6			5			1	
		5	6		3	4		
8	1	4	7		5	3	9	6
		9		1		7		
			9	3	4			
4	8		5	7	2		6	3
3								5

3	2	1		5		9	4	7
7	8			1			6	5
		6	7		4	1		
5	4	9				7	8	6
			9		6			
1		5		6		4		2
	3		2		7		5	
2		7		4		8		3

E-5

			6	9		8		
	7	4		8	1	3	6	
8	1		7		5		4	
	8	5				7		4
2	3						8	6
4		9				5	2	
	9		5		3		1	7
	4	1	9	7		6	5	
		2		4	6			

E-6

	7		4		9		1	
			3		5			
6			8	1	2			3
	6	7		8		9	4	
			5	4	6			
1	4	3				5	6	8
		5				4		
8	3		7	2	4		5	9
4		9				2		7

6	5	9		1		2	8	
1				5			3	
2			8				1	
			1	3	5		7	
8			9					2
		3		7	8	6	4	
3		2			9			4
					1	8		
		8	7	6				

	6			7	2			1
8			1	3	6	5		
		3	4					
2			6	5			3	
		6			7		1	
			2			8	6	4
9		7		8	4			
		8			9		7	
			7	2	1		8	3

M-9

					9	2		
5	4			3		1		
		8		5	7			4
	5			8				3
9		3		4	6	8		
1			3				4	
	7		4					
3	6	1		7	9		8	
				6			3	7

M-10

7			8	4		2		5
	3		1	5		4		
		5		6			7	
	9			3	4	5	8	
	2	8	7			9		3
5		3	9			6		
		4	5	2			9	
		9	4		8			
8					1	7		

M-11

						7		
3	9		7		8	5	4	
8	6			5	4			
9		6		4	7			
1	3	4	2				9	
	5	8	1		9			4
5	4		9	2	3			8
				7		9		5
					1		3	

M-12

8	9		7	6	4	5		
	4		3					9
3	2	7	9					
	8			5	3		1	
			6		1			
6							4	
7			4	9		8	3	
		9			8	2	7	

H-13

2		8			7	3		
	4		8					
	7					9	6	
	6	5						
	3	1				6		5
	2	9	6				7	
6	9						2	1
				5	1			6

H-14

					9			
1	5			3		7		4
	9		1		8			
9								5
		5		1	3			7
8		6						
4	2	3					8	
	1	7		5				
5						1		

			9	8				2
	9					3		5
					4	9		
				1	6			
8		2	7				4	
			3					
2	3		5					
		1	6	2	3	5	8	
7	8							

					1	5	6	
		3		9				8
							7	
5			6					
					7	2	8	
		8						4
9				8	4			3
	6	4		3		1		
7		2	1		9			

H-17

4		7				8		2
		5	3		8			
9			6			5		
8	1			9			5	7
2			4					6
5								
			7	8	3			5
		4						3
				1				

H-18

4			1	2			5	6
9							2	
				5			9	7
1						2		
7			3		5	6		
			7		2			1
	3							
	9	7	5					
				8		5	1	

	8	9	4		1	7	3	
4		2				8		9
7	3		8		6		5	4
8		3		4		6		1
			3		9			
2		5		6		9		3
1	2		7		4		9	8
9		4				1		7
	7	8	9		2	4	6	

				8		7		
				5	4			3
5					2	9		
			4			2	3	
	9		5		6		1	
					7			
		2	1		5			
	5	4		7				
			6	2			5	9

Ans-E1

7	2	3	8	4	6	1	5	9
6	1	5	3	9	2	4	7	8
8	4	9	7	1	5	6	3	2
3	7	8	6	5	4	9	2	1
1	9	4	2	8	7	3	6	5
2	5	6	9	3	1	8	4	7
5	6	1	4	7	9	2	8	3
4	8	7	1	2	3	5	9	6
9	3	2	5	6	8	7	1	4

Ans-E4

3	2	1	6	5	8	9	4	7
7	8	4	3	1	9	2	6	5
9	5	6	7	2	4	1	3	8
5	4	9	1	3	2	7	8	6
6	7	2	4	8	5	3	1	9
8	1	3	9	7	6	5	2	4
1	9	5	8	6	3	4	7	2
4	3	8	2	9	7	6	5	1
2	6	7	5	4	1	8	9	3

Ans-E2

3	2	7	1	5	8	9	4	6
6	1	9	4	3	7	5	8	2
5	4	8	9	6	2	7	1	3
1	8	6	5	7	4	3	2	9
4	3	2	6	8	9	1	5	7
9	7	5	3	2	1	4	6	8
7	6	4	2	1	3	8	9	5
8	5	1	7	9	6	2	3	4
2	9	3	8	4	5	6	7	1

Ans-E5

5	2	3	6	9	4	8	7	1
9	7	4	2	8	1	3	6	5
8	1	6	7	3	5	2	4	9
1	8	5	3	6	2	7	9	4
2	3	7	4	5	9	1	8	6
4	6	9	8	1	7	5	2	3
6	9	8	5	2	3	4	1	7
3	4	1	9	7	8	6	5	2
7	5	2	1	4	6	9	3	8

Ans-E3

1	5	3	8	4	7	6	2	9
9	4	8	2	6	1	5	3	7
7	6	2	3	5	9	8	1	4
2	7	5	6	9	3	4	8	1
8	1	4	7	2	5	3	9	6
6	3	9	4	1	8	7	5	2
5	2	6	9	3	4	1	7	8
4	8	1	5	7	2	9	6	3
3	9	7	1	8	6	2	4	5

Ans-E6

3	7	2	4	6	9	8	1	5
9	8	1	3	7	5	6	2	4
6	5	4	8	1	2	7	9	3
5	6	7	1	8	3	9	4	2
2	9	8	5	4	6	3	7	1
1	4	3	2	9	7	5	6	8
7	2	5	9	3	1	4	8	6
8	3	6	7	2	4	1	5	9
4	1	9	6	5	8	2	3	7

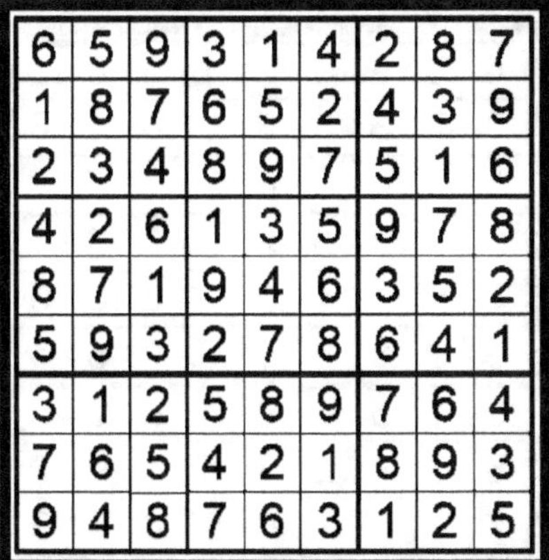

Ans-M7

6	5	9	3	1	4	2	8	7
1	8	7	6	5	2	4	3	9
2	3	4	8	9	7	5	1	6
4	2	6	1	3	5	9	7	8
8	7	1	9	4	6	3	5	2
5	9	3	2	7	8	6	4	1
3	1	2	5	8	9	7	6	4
7	6	5	4	2	1	8	9	3
9	4	8	7	6	3	1	2	5

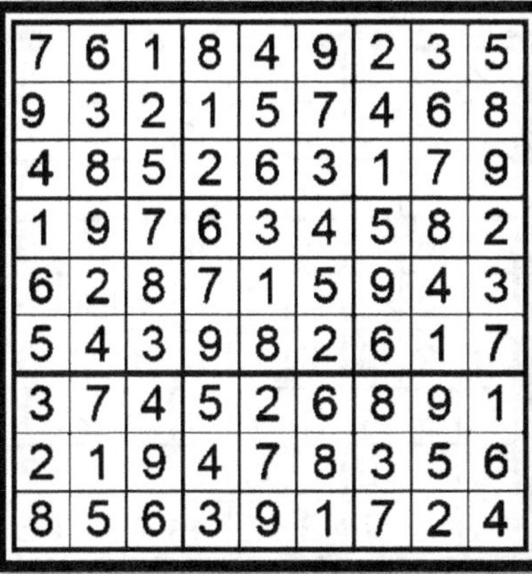

Ans-M10

7	6	1	8	4	9	2	3	5
9	3	2	1	5	7	4	6	8
4	8	5	2	6	3	1	7	9
1	9	7	6	3	4	5	8	2
6	2	8	7	1	5	9	4	3
5	4	3	9	8	2	6	1	7
3	7	4	5	2	6	8	9	1
2	1	9	4	7	8	3	5	6
8	5	6	3	9	1	7	2	4

Ans-M8

4	6	5	8	7	2	3	9	1
8	9	2	1	3	6	5	4	7
7	1	3	4	9	5	6	2	8
2	4	1	6	5	8	7	3	9
3	8	6	9	4	7	2	1	5
5	7	9	2	1	3	8	6	4
9	2	7	3	8	4	1	5	6
1	3	8	5	6	9	4	7	2
6	5	4	7	2	1	9	8	3

Ans-M11

4	1	5	6	9	2	7	8	3
3	9	2	7	1	8	5	4	6
8	6	7	3	5	4	1	2	9
9	2	6	8	4	7	3	5	1
1	3	4	2	6	5	8	9	7
7	5	8	1	3	9	2	6	4
5	4	1	9	2	3	6	7	8
2	8	3	4	7	6	9	1	5
6	7	9	5	8	1	4	3	2

Ans-M9

7	3	6	8	1	4	9	2	5
5	4	9	6	3	2	1	7	8
2	1	8	9	5	7	3	6	4
6	5	4	2	8	1	7	9	3
9	2	3	7	4	6	8	5	1
1	8	7	3	9	5	2	4	6
8	7	5	4	2	3	6	1	9
3	6	1	5	7	9	4	8	2
4	9	2	1	6	8	5	3	7

Ans-M12

8	9	1	7	6	4	5	2	3
5	4	6	3	1	2	7	8	9
3	2	7	9	8	5	1	6	4
9	8	4	2	5	3	6	1	7
2	7	3	6	4	1	9	5	8
6	1	5	8	7	9	3	4	2
7	5	2	4	9	6	8	3	1
4	6	9	1	3	8	2	7	5
1	3	8	5	2	7	4	9	6

Ans-H13

2	5	8	9	6	7	3	1	4
9	4	6	8	1	3	7	5	2
1	7	3	5	4	2	9	6	8
7	6	5	1	3	4	2	8	9
8	3	1	7	2	9	6	4	5
4	2	9	6	8	5	1	7	3
6	9	4	3	7	8	5	2	1
5	1	2	4	9	6	8	3	7
3	8	7	2	5	1	4	9	6

Ans-H16

4	8	9	3	7	1	5	6	2
2	7	3	5	9	6	4	1	8
1	5	6	8	4	2	3	7	9
5	4	7	6	2	8	9	3	1
3	9	1	4	5	7	2	8	6
6	2	8	9	1	3	7	5	4
9	1	5	7	8	4	6	2	3
8	6	4	2	3	5	1	9	7
7	3	2	1	6	9	8	4	5

Ans-H14

3	6	4	5	7	9	2	1	8
1	5	8	2	3	6	7	9	4
7	9	2	1	4	8	6	5	3
9	3	1	6	8	7	4	2	5
2	4	5	9	1	3	8	6	7
8	7	6	4	2	5	9	3	1
4	2	3	7	9	1	5	8	6
6	1	7	8	5	2	3	4	9
5	8	9	3	6	4	1	7	2

Ans-H17

4	3	7	1	5	9	8	6	2
1	6	5	3	2	8	7	9	4
9	2	8	6	4	7	5	3	1
8	1	3	2	9	6	4	5	7
2	7	9	4	3	5	1	8	6
5	4	6	8	7	1	3	2	9
6	9	1	7	8	3	2	4	5
7	8	4	5	6	2	9	1	3
3	5	2	9	1	4	6	7	8

Ans-H15

1	6	3	9	8	5	4	7	2
4	9	8	2	6	7	3	1	5
5	2	7	1	3	4	9	6	8
3	5	4	8	1	6	7	2	9
8	1	2	7	5	9	6	4	3
6	7	9	3	4	2	8	5	1
2	3	6	5	7	8	1	9	4
9	4	1	6	2	3	5	8	7
7	8	5	4	9	1	2	3	6

Ans-H18

4	7	8	1	2	9	3	5	6
9	5	6	8	7	3	1	2	4
3	1	2	4	5	6	8	9	7
1	4	3	6	9	8	2	7	5
7	2	9	3	1	5	6	4	8
6	8	5	7	4	2	9	3	1
5	3	1	2	6	4	7	8	9
8	9	7	5	3	1	4	6	2
2	6	4	9	8	7	5	1	3

5	8	9	4	2	1	7	3	6
4	6	2	5	7	3	8	1	9
7	3	1	8	9	6	2	5	4
8	9	3	2	4	5	6	7	1
6	1	7	3	8	9	5	4	2
2	4	5	1	6	7	9	8	3
1	2	6	7	5	4	3	9	8
9	5	4	6	3	8	1	2	7
3	7	8	9	1	2	4	6	5

Ans-E19

4	3	6	9	8	1	7	2	5
1	2	9	7	5	4	6	8	3
5	7	8	3	6	2	9	4	1
6	1	5	4	9	8	2	3	7
2	9	7	5	3	6	8	1	4
8	4	3	2	1	7	5	9	6
9	6	2	1	4	5	3	7	8
3	5	4	8	7	9	1	6	2
7	8	1	6	2	3	4	5	9

Ans-H20

10 Sudoku Tips and Tricks That'll Help You Solve Faster: -

i. Know where to start solving.
ii. Look for single candidates.
iii. Work on your scanning techniques.
iv. Don't focus too long in the one place.
v. Keep the momentum going.
vi. Make use of pencil marking.
vii. Look for naked pairs.
viii. Look for hidden pairs.
ix. Work your way through more advanced Sudoku strategies.
x. Don't guess – use the process of elimination.